ה

Shabbos and Yom Tov

דברי תורה

for Children

Based on the teachings of the Lubavitcher Rebbe

Written in a clear and simple style
for children to understand,
yet enjoyable for all ages to read

Volume 1

By Rabbi Yekusiel Goldstein

Shabbos and *Yom Tov*
Divrei Torah
for Children

Rimon Publishing
Brooklyn, New York
RimonPublishing@gmail.com

Cover Art: "Shabbat" by Albert Benaroya @www.albertbenaroya.com
Illustration Credit: Eli Brenenson; Yechiel Offner www.yoffner.com;
C.M. Goldstein; S.M. Einstein; H. Feldman;
Rivkie Bukiet copyright and reprinted with permission from
Chabad.org; Daniella Fund via JewishVisual.com

Edited together with Rabbi Adam Epstein

Acknowledgements
Mr. Albert Benaroya for permission to publish his art on the cover
Rabbi Yechiel Offner for making some of his drawings available
Rabbi Yanky Goldstein for all his time and effort!
Chabad.org for making some of their parsha pictures available
Rabbi Adam Epstein for editing Sefer Bereishis and general feedback
Rabbi Shua Hecht for dedicating many hours to the preparation
of this book.
Kehos Publications whose publications were used in the preparation
of this book.

Table of Contents

Shabbos and Yom Tov

דברי תורה

for Children

Volume 1

בְּרֵאשִׁית

The Last Minute

Hashem created the world in six days and rested on the seventh. Rashi writes that Hashem finished the last details of the world at the exact moment that *shabbos* began.

Question - Hashem could have finished creating the world much earlier, why did He wait until the last minute to finish the final details of creation?

Answer - Hashem used every moment of the six days of creation, up until the last second, to show us how we must use out our time. Every day that Hashem gives us, is for the purpose of serving Hashem with His *Torah* and *mitzvos*. Not just every day, but every **hour**, every **minute**, and even every **second** we are alive, Hashem gave us that moment to be used for the purpose of serving Him. We can be just like Hashem using out every moment of every day.

Lesson - A person might think, "We don't have the Avos and Moshe *Rabeinu* and we are so far from the times of the *Beis Hamikdash* where we saw the *Shechina* revealed. How is it possible for us to serve Hashem in these last moments of *golus*? How is it possible that we are going to bring the *geula*?!"

The Rebbe told us that we are the last generation of *golus* who will bring the *geula*. In this week's *parsha* Hashem shows us how precious the last moments can be. Since we are living in these last moments of *golus*, it must be for a purpose. Just like Hashem completed the whole creation in the last few moments, so too, in the last moments of *golus* it is us who will do the last few *mitzvos* to tip the scale and bring the *geula*!

(Based on Likutei Sichos vol. 5 p. 34)

3

To Love and to Care

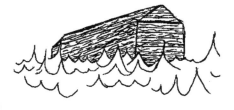

The people in Noach's generation did many sins, yet Noach was a *tzadik* and found favor in Hashem's eyes. Hashem told Noach, the only *tzadik*, that He would bring a *mabul* to destroy the world, and Noach and his family will be saved.

Question - In the *Haftorah* the *mabul* is called "the Waters of Noach - מֵי נֹחַ". That makes it seem as if the *mabul* was his fault. How could that be, if Noach was such a *tzadik* that Hashem saved him from the *mabul*? Why is the *mabul* named after him?

Answer - The *mabul* is named after Noach because he didn't *daven* to Hashem to save the people of his generation. Although Noach was a *tzadik*, it was considered a sin that he only cared about himself and not the other people in his generation. It is therefore called "מֵי נֹחַ".

4

Lesson - Sometimes we may look around at our friends and think that we are the best kid in our class. We keep every single *mitzva* and get 100s on all our tests, but that is not good enough! We must also care for and help our friends and all our fellow *Yidden* by encouraging them as well to do the *Torah* and *mitzvos*.

(Based on Likutei Sichos vol. 2 p. 452)

First of All

In this week's *parsha* we learn about the *mitzva* of *bris mila*. This *mitzva* was the <u>first</u> *mitzva* given to  Avraham *Avinu*, the <u>first</u> *Yid*. It is also the <u>first</u> *mitzva* experienced by every *Yiddishe* boy shortly after he is born!

Question - Why was **this** *mitzva* chosen to be first over all the other *mitzvos*?

Answer - There is a special lesson we learn from the *mitzva* of *bris mila* that applies to all the other *mitzvos*.

At the *mitzva* of *bris mila* the little baby getting the *bris* **cries** from pain. The baby cries because he does not appreciate how **special** this *mitzva* is. If the baby would understand the greatness of the *mitzva*, he would be excited about that and not feel the pain.

The same idea applies to every *mitzva*. Sometimes it can **seem** difficult for us to do a *mitzva* like schlepping something for our father, listening right away to our mother, or *davening* in *shul*. The truth is, it is only difficult for us if we don't realize how great the *mitzva* is, just like the baby who cries during the *mitzva* of *bris mila*. If we stop and think about the greatness of the *mitzva* we are doing, we will feel excitement and happiness of doing what Hashem wants. Then, no *mitzva* can ever be too difficult to do!

(Based on sicha 22 Iyar 5702)

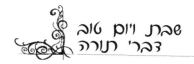
וַיֵּרָא

They all Believe

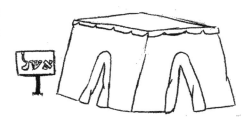

Avraham *Avinu* did the *mitzva* of *hachnasas orchim* to the extent that he would even invite guests who served *avoda zara!* When the guests were done eating, they would thank Avraham *Avinu*, but he would tell them to instead thank Hashem. Avraham *Avinu* loved serving guests in order to teach them about Hashem, who provides all our needs.

The *Midrash* says that if a guest did not want to praise Hashem, Avraham *Avinu* would charge him a lot of money for the meal he had provided. Avraham *Avinu* would explain, "It is hard to find food in the desert, so it is really expensive". Not wanting to pay so much, the guest would agree to praise Hashem.

Question - Avraham *Avinu's* goal in charging the guests was to get them to praise Hashem. Is it considered praising Hashem if the guest was **forced** and didn't mean what he said?

Answer - Every person, even a *goy*, has a *mitzva* to believe in Hashem. (Hashem creates everyone capable of understanding and praising Him). Avraham *Avinu* did all he could to teach people about the One Hashem. When Avraham *Avinu* would meet a person who wasn't interested in hearing about Hashem, he would "shake him up" by charging him with an expensive bill. Once the guest was surprised in such a way, he forgot about his own ego and became ready to praise Hashem.

Lesson - Every person wants to learn about Hashem. We must never be too shy to teach them about Hashem. When the neighbor asks us how we are doing we should answer "Fine, Thank G-D!", or when the mailman asks us how our day was, we should be proud to say "Thank G-D great!" If we say it with our full heart, they in turn will praise Hashem too!

(Based on Likutei Sichos vol. 15 p. 122)

שבת ויום טוב
דברי תורה

✦ וַיֵּרָא - כ' חֶשְׁוָן ✦

For Hashem's Sake

Chof Cheshvan is the birthday of the Rebbe Rashab.

When the Rebbe Rashab was about four or five years old, he went to his *zeide* the Tzemach Tzedek to get a *bracha* for his birthday. When he entered his *zeide's* room, he began to cry.

His *zeide,* the Tzemach Tzedek, asked him why he was crying. The Rebbe Rashab answered: "In cheder we learned, in *Parshas Vayera*, that Hashem revealed Himself to Avraham *Avinu*. Why doesn't Hashem reveal Himself to me?"

The Tzemach Tzedek answered: "When a *Yid*, a Tzaddik, who is 99 years old, recognizes that he must get a *bris mila*, he deserves that Hashem reveal Himself to him."

The Rebbe teaches us, that there is a lesson we can learn from this story:

It used to be that in order to get a child to *daven* or learn *Torah*, the child would have to be rewarded a prize or candy. After this story of the Rebbe Rashab took place, children are able to *Daven* and learn לִשְׁמָהּ - just for Hashem's sake, not for anything else! A child can even **cry** because he wants to see Hashem, just like the Rebbe Rashab! They do this out of their strong love for Hashem.

(Based on Likutei Sichos vol. 15 p. 129)

שבת ויום טוב
דברי תורה

✦ חַיֵּי שָׂרָה ✦

True Life

This week's *parsha* חַיֵּי שָׂרָה, "Life of Sara," has a misleading name because only the first *possuk* actually mentions Sara's **life**. The second *possuk* already speaks about Sara's passing away. Why is the name of the *parsha* חַיֵּי שָׂרָה, the **life** of Sara?

Answer - 'True life' of a *Yid* never ends, even with death. When a *Yid* sees his children and grandchildren continuing to live in the way that **he** lived, the way of Hashem, then his life continues on, even after he passes away!

In this week's *parsha*, right after Sara *Imeinu* passed away, the *Torah* tells us how Yitzchak married Rivka, who lived a life of *Torah* and *mitzvos* like Sara *Imeinu*. The three miracles that happened by Sara *Imeinu*

also happened to Rivka! Thus, in this week's *parsha*, even though Sara passes away, we see how her life, the חַיֵּי שָׂרָה, continued on.

Lesson - *Moshiach* will come very soon and we will be reunited with our ancestors who passed away. In these last few moments of *golus*, we can make their lives continue on by living the way they did, a life of *Torah* and *mitzvos*.

(Based on Likutei Sichos vol. 15 p. 145)

תּוֹלְדוֹת

Guard your Mouth

Yitzchak was getting old and he wanted to give Eisav special *berachos*. In the end, he gave the *berachos* to Yaakov. Rashi writes that Hashem actually made Yitzchak blind so that he would think that Yaakov was Eisav and give him the *berachos*.

Question - Instead of making Yitzchak blind, Hashem could have just told Yitzchak that Eisav was a rasha and did not deserve the *berachos*. Why did Hashem have to make Yitzchak blind?

Answer - Speaking *lashon hara* is a terrible sin, so much so that **even Hashem** didn't want to do it! Therefore, in order to make sure that Yaakov gets the *berachos*, Hashem made Yitzchak blind, rather than telling him that Eisav was a rasha.

Lesson - Hashem was careful not to speak *lashon hara* about a rasha - such as Eisav – and rather chose to make Yitzchak blind! We must certainly be very careful to only speak good about others and **never** say anything bad about another *Yid*!

(Based on Likutei Sichos vol. 15 p. 215)

☀ וַיֵּצֵא ☀

Keeping your Head Above

Yaakov ran away from his brother Eisav and traveled to *Charan*. On the way, he stopped off and slept on Har Hamoria. Before Yaakov went to sleep, he put stones around his head to protect himself.

Question - If Yaakov was trying to protect himself, shouldn't he have put stones around his **whole body**, not just his **head**?

Answer - Yaakov put the stones around his head not only to protect his body, but also to protect his *neshama* and mind.

Yaakov was on the way to his tricky and sly uncle, Lavan. Until now he was in Yeshiva, only involved in *Torah* and *mitzvos*. Once he would go to *Charan*, he would have to start dealing with worldly matters instead of only learning *Torah*. Yaakov wanted to do this with his **hands** alone and not have his **head**, **mind**, and *neshama*, involved. Yaakov put the stones only around his head because his main concern was that his **head** always stay connected and focused on *Torah* and *mitzvos*.

Story - A businessman once asked the Rebbe Rashab about his business of selling boots. The businessman was so involved in his questions, that the Rebbe turned to him and said, "I have heard of people putting their **feet** into their boots. I haven't heard yet of people putting their **head** into their boots!"

Lesson - We should be excited and involved with all our might when doing *Torah* and *mitzvos*! When we are doing things like playing games, eating and sleeping we should get involved only with our body, hands and feet. Our head and our *neshama* should always stay focused on Hashem and His *Torah* and *mitzvos*.

(Based on Likutei Sichos vol. 1 p. 61)

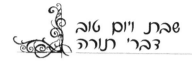
וַיִּשְׁלַח

Hashem's Love

Before greeting his brother Eisav, Yaakov met Eisav's *malach* and fought with him. At the end Yaakov was the winner! The *malach* was only able to hurt Yaakov's thigh, the גיד הנשה. To remember this victory, we -Yaakov's children- don't eat the גיד הנשה (the small vein by the thigh) when shechting an animal.

Question – The story of the גיד הנשה, is only one small detail of the fight between Yaakov and the *malach*. Shouldn't there be a better way to remember Yaakov's victory? The vein also highlights how Yaakov was hurt by the *malach* and not completely victorious.

Answer - The *Torah* chose the גיד הנשה to remember Yaakov's victory because the *Torah* wants to show us how precious the *Yidden* are to Hashem. Only one little vein from one single *Yid* was hurt, yet it was enough of a big deal for Hashem to make us remember it.

This shows us how much Hashem loves and cares about every *Yid*. Every detail of a *Yid*'s life, even his *gashmiyus* (physical things) is important to Hashem!

Lesson - We can learn from this two lessons: 1) To act just like Hashem and show our love and care to every single *Yid*, even to care about the little details of their *gashmiyus*. 2) Just like Hashem cares about every detail in our life, let us show our love back to  Hashem and do His *mitzvos* with love, caring about every single detail!

(Based on Likutei Sichos vol. 30 p. 148)

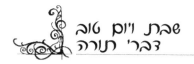

וַיֵּשֶׁב

How are You?

Yosef was kidnapped by his brothers and sold to Potifar in *Mitzrayim*. Over there, he was falsely accused of acting inappropriately and sent to prison. One morning, Yosef saw the chief butler and chief baker and asked them, "Why do you look so sad today?" They answered that they both had puzzling dreams which they couldn't explain. Yosef helped them to interpret their dreams.

Yosef was kidnapped, sold as a slave, wrongly thrown into prison, and he was away from his father for over ten years! Can you imagine how you would feel? It would make sense for him to be sad and not be able to care for anyone else. Instead, he looked around to see if anyone else was having a hard day or needed help.

Lesson - We must care about our friends and the people around us and try to help them out in whatever way we can. Even if we may be having a bad day or our own problems, we should take a lesson from Yosef to care about others in the best way possible.

(Based on shabbos Parshas Mikeitz 5734)

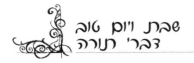
שבת ויום טוב
דברי תורה

חֲנוּכָּה

The Spiritual War

There are a lot of exciting things during *Chanuka*: parties, games of dreidel, gelt, and donuts! When the *Gemara* asks, "What is *Chanuka*?", the *Gemara* answers that the main part of *Chanuka* was actually the miracle of the *Chashmona'im* finding the jug of pure olive oil. This is what one should primarily remember when lighting the Menorah.

Question – There are many feats and miracles in the *Chanuka* story to remember, like the war of the Macabees against the Greeks or the courage of the *Yidden* standing up to the decrees against keeping *shabbos* and learning *Torah*. Why aren't any of these remembered as the main aspect of *Chanuka*?

Answer - The war of the Greeks was primarily a war against our *neshamos*. The Greeks only wanted to stop the *Yidden* from keeping *Torah* and *mitzvos* as a result of **Hashem** telling us to. They said, "Do the *mitzvos*, but don't call it **Hashem's** *mitzvos*. Learn *Torah*, but don't call it **Hashem's** *Torah*.

The goal of their war was to take away our connection to Hashem. When they came to the *Beis Hamikdash* they did not **destroy** the oil, rather they broke the *Kohen Gadol*'s seal to made it **impure**. Rituals like lighting the Menora did not bother them as long as it was not something **heilik** and used for serving **Hashem**.

When we remember the miracle of *Chanuka* and celebrate our victory over the Greeks, we remember the miracle of finding the **pure** oil. The seal of the *Kohen Gadol* shows the victory of the *neshama*, the **הייליקייט,** and our connection to Hashem.

נשמה

(Based on Likutei Sichos vol. 25 p. 237)

23

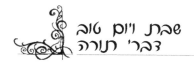
מִקֵּץ

The Power of Teshuva

During the seven years of hunger, Yosef's brothers went down to *Mitzrayim* to get food from the ruler of *Mitzrayim*, not knowing it was Yosef.

When the brothers arrived, Yosef accused them of being spies. They immediately realized that this was happening for a reason. There must have been something they did wrong that they had to do *teshuva* for.

They remembered how 22 years back they acted very cruel to their brother Yosef. Now Hashem was repaying them for their act. They immediately did *teshuva* and regretted their actions.

In the *teshuva* of the brothers we find a few remarkable points:

א) <u>We see the greatness of the שבטים</u>:

1. They were able to feel bad and do *teshuva* for what they did 22 years earlier!
2. This was the only *teshuva* they needed. That means that in the past 22 years, the brothers did not sin at all!

ב) <u>We see that their *teshuva* had an immediate effect</u>:

1. Yosef promised to imprison all of them, but in the end he only imprisoned Shimon. Even then, Yosef released him shortly thereafter.
2. Eventually, Yaakov and his entire family were saved from hunger and reunited with Yosef!

(Based on sicha 5th night of Chanuka 5747)

וַיִּגַּשׁ

True Bitachon

After many years of being separated from his brothers, Yosef revealed himself to them. Yosef then sent them back to *Eretz Kanaan* to bring Yaakov down to *Mitzrayim*. Yosef's invitation to his father included two delicacies of
Mitzrayim: 1) aged wine, and 2) split beans.

Question - What was the significance in Yosef sending **these** two foods?

Answer - Each of these foods was hinting a special message to Yaakov:

<u>The split beans</u> - Yosef knew that Yaakov would be delighted that, Boruch Hashem, he was alive. At the same time Yaakov might be upset at the brothers for causing him so many years of pain. Yosef sent this food to hint: just like one must first **break** and **split** beans to turn them into a **delicacy**, so too Yosef had to be

26

separated from his family before something **good** would become of him. As a result of being in *Mitzrayim*, Yosef was able to save the whole world from the hunger!

The aged wine represents that all the years Yosef was away, he still had *bitachon* in Hashem that one day he will be reunited with his family. Yosef prepared wine long ago for the time when he would use it to celebrate with his father and family.

Lesson - We can learn from Yosef how strong our *bitachon* in Hashem should be. Even though we have been in *golus* for so many years, we must prepare and be ready for *Moshiach*'s coming at any moment!

(Based on Likutei Sichos vol. 10 p. 157)

עֲשָׂרָה בְּטֵבֵת

*Let's **not** go to Golus*

On עֲשָׂרָה בְּטֵבֵת we fast because on this day, "סָמַךְ מֶלֶךְ בָּבֶל אֶל יְרוּשָׁלַיִם" - Nevuchadnetzar, the king of בָּבֶל, surrounded the city of *Yerusholayim*. He did not let any *Yid* go in or out of the city for two and a half years, after which he broke into the city and destroyed the *Beis Hamikdash*.

Question – Why does the *possuk* use the word "סָמַךְ", which can also mean Nevuchadnetzar "**supported**" *Yerusholayim*, when desciribing this sad event?

Answer - The reason for the destruction of the *Beis Hamikdash* was שִׂנְאַת חִנָם, hatred between *Yidden*.

28

Nevuchadnetzar was giving the *Yidden* a message by locking them in the city **all together** that, "If you want to keep your *Beis Hamikdash*, then stick **together** with *ahavas Yisroel*!" The *possuk* says סָמַךְ, since Nevuchadnetzar was really **supporting** the *Yidden* and showing them how to do *teshuva*.

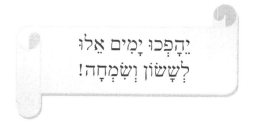

Let us have extra *ahavas Yisroel* to merit the rebuilding of the third *Beis Hamikdash*, Amein!

(Based on Likutei Sichos vol. 25 p. 267)

נֶהֶפְכוּ יָמִים אֵלּוּ
לְשָׂשׂוֹן וְשִׂמְחָה!

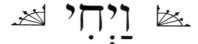

וַיְחִי

Chazak!

The last *possuk* of *chumash* bereishis finishes off, "וַיָּמָת יוֹסֵף... וַיִּישֶׂם בָּאָרוֹן בְּמִצְרָיִם," that Yosef passed away and was buried in *Mitzrayim*. Following these words, everyone calls out, "חֲזַק חֲזַק וְנִתְחַזֵּק!!!" "Be strong, be strong, and may we be strengthened!"

Question - Yosef's passing away and being buried in *Mitzrayim* seems to be a sad thing. Why then do we make a joyous announcement, "חֲזַק חֲזַק וְנִתְחַזֵּק!!!"?!

Answer - Yosef's brothers found out about the upcoming *golus* mitzrayim, which would begin with Yosef's passing. The brothers thought, "How will we make it through this dark *golus*? What will give us the "חִיזוּק", the strength?"

30

The *Torah* therefore tells the *Yidden*, although "וַיָּמָת יוֹסֵף," Yosef passed away, nevertheless, " וַיִּישֶׂם בָּאָרוֹן בְּמִצְרָיִם", he is staying with you in *golus*, giving you the "חִיזוּק" and strength to make it through. In the end you will go out of *golus* together **with** Yosef! When we hear these words, "וַיִּישֶׂם בָּאָרוֹן בְּמִצְרָיִם", that Yosef is staying with us in *golus*,

we call out " חזק חזק ונתחזק!", since these words give us true strength!

(Based on Likutei Sichos vol. 25 p. 476)

31

שְׁמוֹת

Easy but Hard

The Egyptians made the *Yidden* work very hard. The *Torah* says, "The Egyptians enslaved the *Yidden* with backbreaking work". The *Gemara* explains that the "backbreaking work" was that they made the women do men's work and the men do women's work.

Question – We can understand how a woman doing men's work, like **building** and carrying **heavy loads**, is backbreaking. But why is it backbreaking for a man to do women's work such as sewing and cleaning?

Answer - It goes against a person's nature to do work that he is not used to. Although the lighter tasks may have been physically easier for the men, it was considered backbreaking because they were not used to it.

Lesson - Our *neshama* is used to doing *mitzvos* and not aveiros. Listening to the *yetzer hara* to not do a *mitzva*

32

or to do an *aveira*, is **backbreaking** for the *neshama* because it is not used to such behavior.

Doing a *mitzva* can **seem** harder than just skipping it completely, we learn from this week's *parsha* that **not** doing the *mitzvos* is actually backbreaking for the *neshama*.

Let us comfort our *neshama* the way it **really** wants and do as many *mitzvos* as we can!

(Based on Likutei Sichos vol. 1 p. 117)

33

וָאֵרָא

Who's the Boss?

Hashem brought ten *makos* on *Mitzrayim*. The *makos* served two purposes; firstly, they were a punishment to Paroh and the *Mitzriyim* for enslaving the *Yidden* for so many years. Secondly, Paroh kept saying that he is a god and Hashem was teaching him that He is the One in charge and not Paroh or any of the "gods" that they believed in.

It was specifically by the *maka* of *barad*, hail, that Paroh announced, "ה' הַצַּדִּיק, וַאֲנִי וְעַמִּי הָרְשָׁעִים", "Hashem is the Righteous One, and me and my nation are the wicked ones".

Question - Why was it specifically by the *maka* of *barad* that Paroh recognized Hashem as the righteous one, why not by any of the other *makos*? What is special about this *maka*?

Answer - One of the idols of *Mitzrayim* was the *Nilus* River. The *Nilus* watered all their fields and gave

them all the food that they needed. The Egyptians would therefore say, "There is no one above in the *shomayim*, we don't need anything from Hashem above, no rain, no *berachos*, everything comes from our river!"

When Hashem wanted to show Paroh that He is the true boss, he brought hail, which comes from the *shomayim*. This was showing Paroh, how he **is** dependent on the *shomayim* and on the *berachos* from Hashem. When Paroh didn't do *teshuva*, Hashem transformed the rain into hail and used the *shomayim* as a means to destroy his fields and all his riches. This will surely teach Paroh a lesson that there is a Creator in the *shomayim* and that he is dependent on Hashem. We see that Paroh got the message when he announced, "Hashem *HaTzadik*-Hashem is the Righteous One."

Lesson - From this *parsha* we learn to recognize that everything comes from Hashem. Like this, we will always be thankful for the good that Hashem gives us. We show our thankfulness to Hashem when we say a *bracha* before and after we eat and by having a lot of *kavana* when we *daven*.

(Based on Parshas vaera 5702)

 וָאֵרָא - כ"ד טֵבֵת

Turn the Light On

כ"ד טֵבֵת is the *yahrtzeit* of the Alter Rebbe. Chassidus explains that there is a special connection between a Yom Tov or a special day with the *parsha* of that week.

Question - כ"ד טֵבֵת often occurs in *Parshas Va'eira*. What is the connection between the Alter Rebbe and *Parshas Va'eira*?

Answer - The connection is actually found in the name of the Alter Rebbe and the *parsha*. The Alter Rebbe's first name, Schneur, comes from the words שְׁנֵי אוֹר (two lights). The Alter Rebbe taught **two lights**, one in נִגְלָה (the revealed part of *Torah*), *Shulchan Aruch*, and the second in נִסְתָּר (the hidden part of *Torah*), Chassidus.

These **two lights** of the Alter Rebbe are hinted in the name of the *parsha*, וָאֵרָא. The letters of וָאֵרָא also spell out אוֹר א.

אור is a hint to the **revealed** light of the Alter Rebbe (the *Shulchan Aruch*), since all the letters of אור are **clearly** seen in the word וָאֵרָא.

The last א, is a hint to the **hidden** light of the Alter Rebbe (Chassidus), since only the letter א from the word אור is seen.

Why do we use the word **'אור'-light** to describe the Alter Rebbe's teachings?

When someone doesn't understand something he feels like he is in a **dark** room. Then when he understands it he feels like the **light** was turned on!

The same is true with the Alter Rebbe's teachings. In the *Shulchan Aruch* the Alter Rebbe explains all the *halachos* very **clearly,** with their reasons, so that everyone can understand them well. Also with *Chassidus* the Alter Rebbe explains the *Maamorim* in a very **clear** way so that everyone can fully understand them.

He brings '**Light**' to these two parts of the *Torah*!

(Based on Likutei Sichos vol. 26 p. 40)

The Little Kinderlach

Moshe warned Paroh about the last *makos,* and the *Yidden* started getting ready to leave *Mitzrayim.* One of the things the *Yidden* did to prepare for *yetzias*

Mitzrayim was the *mitzva* of *korban Pesach.* Every *Yid* shechted a sheep that would be big enough for every member in his family, including the small children, to have a part to eat.

Question – We don't find by the other *mitzvos* that children have a part in them just like the adults. Why is the *mitzva* of *korban Pesach* different?

Answer – When the Egyptians threw the babies into the *Nilus*, Hashem made many miracles to save them: The *Nilus* spit them out, the stones fed them, and the ground hid them from the Egyptians. Thus, these babies had a special connection to Hashem!

Whenever we do a *mitzva* we connect to Hashem. The children, who already had a special connection to

Hashem, were able to do the *mitzva* of *korban Pesach* and connect to Hashem in an **even stronger** way than the adults! Therefore, there was a portion of the *korban Pesach* especially for them.

Later on by krias *Yam suf*, the children were the first ones to recognize Hashem, even before the adults! They called out, "This is my Hashem! - זֶה אֵ-לִי!" Since they recognized Hashem from when they were little babies.

Lesson - By *yetzias Mitzrayim*, the children were the first ones to recognize Hashem and to prepare for the *geula*, and the same thing is now by the final *geula*. The children are the ones at the lead to prepare for the *geula* and they will be the first to recognize Hashem at the coming of *Moshiach*!

(Based on sicha Rosh Chodesh Nisan 5740)

בְּשַׁלַּח

Stop, Drop, and Care

After 210 years of hard work, the *Yidden* finally left *Mitzrayim*. Paroh regretted setting the *Yidden* free and chased after them. The *Yidden* were standing by the *Yam suf* and the *Mitzriyim* were approaching quickly. The *Yidden* were frightened and didn't know what to do, so they turned to Moshe for help.

Moshe *Rabeinu* cried out to Hashem to help the *Yidden*. Hashem told Moshe, "Why are you crying to me? Now is not a time for *davening*, my children are in danger. Tell the *Yidden* to travel forward!"

Question – Why did Hashem have to first tell Moshe, "Why are you crying to me? My children are in danger"? If the point was that the *Yidden* should go forward, Hashem could have just told Moshe, "Tell the *Yidden* to travel forward!" and that's it.

Answer – Hashem was teaching Moshe, and every *Yid*, a very important lesson. The *Yidden* were in a time of danger and Moshe's mission was to save them. Hashem was telling Moshe, when you go to save a *Yid* you must stop what you are doing and do whatever you can to save him. You must give yourself over with your full attention and can't be busy *davening*.

That is why Hashem said, "Why are you crying to me?" it isn't enough that Moshe will tell the *Yidden* to go forward while he will continue *Davening*, but rather, he must stop whatever he is doing and give himself over **completely** to help the *Yidden* who are now in danger.

Lesson - If we hear or know about another *Yid* who needs help, it may even be another kid in our class, or someone in our family, we must stop whatever we are doing to help them. Even if we are *davening* or doing something else very important, we must stop in order to help the other *Yid*.

(Based on Toras Menachem vol. 25 p. 42)

יִתְרוֹ

Is Egypt Good or Bad?

After 49 days of preparation the *Yidden* stood at Har Sinai for *matan Torah*. Hashem came down to Har Sinai and said: "אָנֹכִי ה'

אֱלֹקֶיךָ..." "I am Hashem your G-d...." The *Midrash* says that the word "אָנֹכִי" is actually an Egyptian word!

Question – The *aseres hadibros* are the base for the whole *Torah*. How is it possible that the **first** word of the **first** commandment is an **Egyptian** word?! Shouldn't it be in לְשׁוֹן הַקּוֹדֶשׁ?

Answer – Hashem chose the word אָנֹכִי, an Egyptian word, as the first word of the *aseres hadibros* to show us what the purpose of the *Torah* is.

The point of the *Torah* is to spread *Torah* and *mitzvos* to the whole world. We shouldn't just stay "locked up" in *kedusha*, to just stay in *shul* all day and forget about the world around us. Rather to use everything we see **in this world** to serve Hashem better.

For example, if you have a yummy snack, you may think that since it's something physical it is considered bad and want to throw it away. But really you can use it for Hashem! Firstly, making a *bracha*, and then, *davening* or learning with the *koach* you got from eating the snack. One can take leather and use it to make a pair of *tefillin*.

That is why the first word of the *aseres hadibros* is אָנֹכִי, in **Egyptian**. The point isn't to **drop** the other languages, but rather to **use** them **for** *kedusha* and for *Torah*.

That is also what Moshe told the *malochim* when they wanted to keep the *Torah* for themselves. He told them, "Did you go down to *Mitzrayim?!* Do you have a *yetzer hara?!* Do you have to do with this world?!" If not, the *Torah* is not for you! It is for the *Yidden* who are **in** this world and use the *gashmiyus* to serve Hashem!

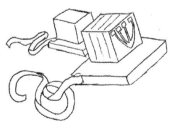

(Based on Likutei Sichos vol. 3 p. 892)

☀ מִשְׁפָּטִים ☀

Just Ask!

In *Parshas Mishpotim* we learn the laws of many *mitzvos*: *eved ivri*, only telling the truth, *hashovas aveida*, and many more *mitzvos*.

One of the *mitzvos* is the *mitzva* of *basar b'chalav*, not to cook milk and meat together.

Question - There are three types of *mitzvos*, עֵדוֹת, חֻקִּים and מִשְׁפָּטִים. מִשְׁפָּטִים are the *mitzvos* that make sense to us. חֻקִּים are the *mitzvos* that we don't understand the reason behind them.

If so, why is the *mitzva* of *basar b'chalav* in **this** *parsha*, מִשְׁפָּטִים? Isn't it one of the חֻקִּים, a *mitzva* that we **don't** understand the reason?

Answer - Hashem put the *mitzva* of *basar b'chalav* in *Parshas* מִשְׁפָּטִים to teach us a very important lesson.

When someone does something without understanding why he is doing it, he does it with less

44

excitement. But when he understands the reason, he does it with much more excitement and enjoyment.

For example, if your mother asks you to carry a box upstairs, you may or may not be excited to do it. But if she tells you that it's for a special surprise party, then you will likely be more excited to do it!

In a similar way the *Torah* put the *mitzva* of *basar b'chalav,* which is one of the חֻקִּים, in *Parshas* מִשְׁפָּטִים, to teach us that even the *mitzvos* that are חֻקִּים and we **don't understand** them, we should try to find a reason and understand them as much as possible. This will cause us to do the *mitzva* with more excitement, as if it was one of the מִשְׁפָּטִים!

Lesson - When we learn about something and don't understand the reason, or we are doing a *mitzva* and don't know why we are doing it, we should ask and try to find out the reason. This way, we will do the *mitzva* with more excitement, happy to do what Hashem wants.

(Based on Likutei Sichos vol. 16 p. 242; vol. 32 p. 179)

תְּרוּמָה

Ready, Set, Go!

In this week's *parsha* we learn about the building of the *mishkan* and the many *keilim* used inside it to do the *avoda*.

One of the *keilim* in the *mishkan* was the holy Aron. It consisted of three boxes, the *kruvim* on top, and had the luchos inside. It also had poles attached to it that were used to carry the Aron around whenever the *Yidden* traveled in the desert.

Question – Everything in the *mishkan* was built 100% exact in every detail, especially in the holiest place in the *mishkan*, the *kodesh hakadashim*.

How is it then that the poles on the side of the Aron were left attached to the Aron **all the time**? It would have made more sense to have the poles put away on the side and only attach them when it was time to travel. Why were they left there all the time?

Answer – The Aron which has the luchos in it, is a sign for a *Yid* who is learning *Torah*. He is in *shul* or *Yeshiva* where he learns all day, just like the Aron with the luchos is always hidden away in the *kodesh hakadashim*. All this *Yid* thinks about is the *Torah* that he learns.

This person might think that since he is busy with the holiest thing in the world, learning *Torah*, then that should be the only thing on his mind. And if someone needs his help he'll have to stop learning, get ready, and after preparing himself will go help the *Yid*.

The Aron **with** the poles teaches him, NO! Even when he is busy learning, he must always be **ready to go out** and bring the words of *Torah* to others. Just like the Aron always has the Poles **attached** to it, **ready to go** whenever and wherever it needs to.

Lesson – Of course we know that it is the right thing to help another *Yid* when they need, no matter what we are doing. But we must keep in mind that this isn't enough. We must always be **ready to go**, as soon as we hear that a *Yid* needs help, we are already 'out the door'!

(Based on Likutei Sichos vol. 16 p. 334)

47

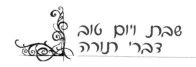

תְּצַוֶּה

When the Bell Rings

One of the *begadim* of the *Kohen Gadol* was the מְעִיל, the long blue robe. On the bottom of the מְעִיל was a pattern of pomegranates and bells.

Question – All the *begadim*, including all their details, were chosen for a special reason. What was the purpose of the bells and the pomegranates on the bottom of the מְעִיל?

Answer - The מְעִיל hints to us how all the *Yidden* are included in the *avoda* of the *Kohen Gadol*.

There are three types of *Yidden*: 1) *Tzadikim*, 2) *Baalei teshuva* and 3) *Resha'im*. Each of them serves Hashem differently.

The *tzadikim* - They serve Hashem in a **humble** and **quiet** way, not showing off how good they are.

The *baalei teshuva* - They are *Yidden* who feel far from Hashem. They feel like they are 'drowning' in their aveiros and want to come back to Hashem. They don't serve Hashem quietly, rather they **cry out** to Hashem and serve Hashem with **excitement**. They are like a drowning

48

person who flaps his arms and legs and makes a lot of noise trying to save himself.

The *resha'im* - They are *Yidden* who sinned and didn't do *teshuva* yet. But the *Gemara* says, "Even Resha'im are full of *mitzvos*, like a **pomegranate** is full of seeds."

Someone may think that when the *Kohen Gadol* did the avoda in the *mishkan* and *Beis Hamikdash*, he only represented the *Tzadikim* who never sinned and serve Hashem in a quiet way, but not the *baalei teshuva* and surely not the *resha'im*. Hashem therefore commanded the *Kohen Gadol* to wear the **bells** and **pomegranates**, to show us that even the *baalei teshuva*, who are louder, similar to the **bells**, and the *resha'im*, who are compared to a **pomegranate**, are included in the *avoda* of the *Kohen Gadol*.

Lesson – Sometimes we may feel a little far from Hashem, or we might not be so careful about doing a certain *mitzva*. We must know that for this short while until we do *teshuva*, Hashem still loves us and cares about us and we are still included in the *avoda* of the *Kohen Gadol*.

(Based on Likutei Sichos vol. 16 p. 336)

☜ פּוּרִים ☞

The Mighty Shepherd

On *Purim* we celebrate the miracle that Hashem saved us from Haman's

terrible decree to destroy all the *Yidden* רחמנא ליצלן!

The *Gemara* asks, why did all the *Yidden* deserve to be destroyed, all the men women and children?

The *Gemara* answers, " מִפְּנֵי שֶׁנֶּהֱנוּ מִסְעוּדָתוֹ שֶׁל אוֹתוֹ רָשָׁע", because they enjoyed the party of Achashveirosh!

Question - How is it possible that just for enjoying the party of Achashveirosh the *Yidden* deserved to be destroyed? Isn't that such a harsh punishment for such a small *aveira*?

Answer - The *Yidden* and the other nations are compared to one sheep amongst seventy wolves. The wolves stand ready to harm the sheep. The only way the

sheep (-the *Yidden*) survives is because it has a powerful shepherd protecting it - Hashem!

What would happen if the sheep told the shepherd, "I don't need you, I am okay without you," the sheep would be killed in an instant!

The same idea was with the *Yidden* and Hashem. When they enjoyed from the party of Achashveirosh, it was as if they were telling Hashem, their faithful shepherd, "We don't need you (*chas veshalom*), we want to enjoy Achashveirosh's party." They were telling their 'Shepherd' to go away. That's why the *Yidden* faced such a harsh decree, to be destroyed רחמנא ליצלן!

Only after the *Yidden* did *teshuva* for a full year, did the shepherd, Hashem, forgive the *Yidden* and made the miracle of *Purim* to save the *Yidden*.

(Based on Likutei Sichos vol. 31 p. 170)

51

⛧ כִּי תִשָּׂא ⛧

Half a Story

After the *Yidden* sinned with the עגל הזהב, the golden calf, Moshe *Rabeinu* davened to Hashem to forgive them.

Hashem told Moshe that every *Yid* should give a *machatzis hashekel*, a half Shekel coin, and that will bring forgiveness for their sin.

Question - We find by all other *mitzvos* that the best way to perform them is in a complete way. For example, all the *keilim* in the *mishkan* could not be **chipped** or **broken**. On *shabbos*, we take a **complete** *challa* for the *seuda*. Why is it then that by the *mitzva* of *machatzis hashekel* the *mitzva* is to give a **half** coin, not a whole coin?

Answer - The חטא העגל was a sin of *avoda zara*. A person can come to serve *avoda zara* (*chas veshalom*)

when he thinks that he is *chas veshalom* 'on his own' and doesn't need Hashem. That is why he serves **other** gods.

To do *teshuva* for this sin, Hashem told the *Yidden* to take *machatizs hashekel*, only **half** a coin, so that when a *Yid* asks, "What can I give as forgiveness? What am I worth?" Hashem answers, "You're only a half," the other half is Hashem! **This** was the forgiveness for the חטא העגל, when they realized that they're only complete **with** Hashem.

Lesson - This shows us in what way a *Yid* and Hashem are connected. It's not just that Hashem is one thing and we are another thing and these two separate things connect to each other, but rather we are **two halves**

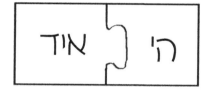

of one thing, and without Hashem we are just not complete!

(Based on Likutei Sichos vol. 3 p. 926)

53

וַיַּקְהֵל

Equally Precious

The *Yidden* donated all the different materials needed to build the *mishkan*. There were those who donated gold and

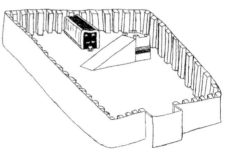

jewelry, while others donated wood and oil. Each person gave according to his ability.

Some *Yidden* may have thought that the donations of the rich were surely more precious to Hashem than the donations of the poor.

Hashem did something to make it clear that all the *Yidden* were equally precious to Him and had an equal part in the *mishkan*. Since it doesn't matter to Hashem as much **what** you are giving, but rather the **kavana** and the **feelings** of the person giving it.

How did Hashem give them this message? When it came time to choose who will build the *mishkan*, Hashem chose Betzalel and Ahaliav to do this special job.

Betzalel came from a great and respected family. He was the grandson of Miriam, and from the *Shevet* of Yehuda. **Ahaliav** on the other hand, was from one of the less honorable shevatim, *Shevet* Don, who was the son of one of the maidservants (-Bilha). Nevertheless, Hashem chose the two of them **together** to build the *mishkan*.

Hashem was telling the *Yidden* that by the building of the *mishkan*, everyone was equal in His eyes - the rich, the poor, the great, and the simple *Yid* - since they all had the same feeling and *kavana*, they were all doing it for the sake of Hashem!

Lesson – When we decide to do something for Hashem, for example to give some of our money to *tzedaka*, or to help another child when he needs our help, what is important is not so much **how much** we are giving, but rather the *kavana* and the **feelings** that we have, that we are doing it for the sake of Hashem.

(Based on Likutei Sichos vol. 31 p. 216)

✦ פְּקוּדֵי - כ"ז אֲדָר ✦

After all, we Need a Rebbe!

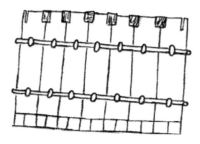

Once the *Yidden* collected all the materials needed for the *mishkan*, Betzalel, Ahaliav, and all the wise men, gathered to build the *mishkan*.

They tried to stand the beams up and put together the *mishkan* but they just couldn't! So they brought everything to Moshe, and, with Hashem's help, Moshe was able to put up the *mishkan*!

In addition, even after the *mishkan* was already built, the *Shechina* still didn't come down. Only after Moshe made a special *tefila*, "יְהִי רָצוֹן שֶׁתִּשְׁרֶה שְׁכִינָה בְּמַעֲשֵׂה יְדֵיכֶם...," he *davened* that Hashem should rest his *Shechina* in the *mishkan* that the *Yidden* made, only then did the *Shechina* finally rest on the *mishkan*.

This teaches us an amazing lesson:

Our mission in this world is to make ourselves, our home, and the entire world a *"mishkan"* for Hashem, a place where Hashem's *Shechina* can rest.

But this is not enough, *Parshas Pikudei* teaches us that in order for this *mishkan* to be complete, our efforts alone are not enough. Even after we did all that we can, we have to come to "Moshe", the Rebbe in each generation. We need his *berachos* to complete the mission and bring the *Shechina* into this world. Through connecting to the Rebbe we succeed in our mission and the Rebbe *bentches* us, " יְהִי

©2019 art770.com

רָצוֹן שֶׁתִּשְׁרֶה שְׁכִינָה בְּמַעֲשֵׂה יְדֵיכֶם."

May we be *zoiche* to spend **this** *shabbos* with the Rebbe, together with the coming of *Moshiach*, now! *Amein*!

(Based on Likutei Sichos vol. 11 p. 172)

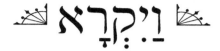

⚡ וַיִּקְרָא ⚡

What we Really Want

Parshas Vayikra speaks about many different *korbanos* and their many *halachos*. One of the *halachos* is that a *korban* must be brought "with his will - לִרְצוֹנוֹ". This means, we cannot force a *Yid* to bring a *korban*.

What happens if someone has to bring a *korban* but he doesn't want to?

The *Gemara* says that we force him until he says that he wants to!

Question - How does that make sense? If we force him, that means he doesn't want to and it's not "לִרְצוֹנוֹ". And if he **does** want to, why are we forcing him?

Answer - Every *Yid* really wants to do Hashem's *mitzvos*, but sometimes the *yetzer hara* tries to stop us from doing the right thing. What do we have to do? We have to get the *yetzer hara* out of the way! Then we can do what we **really** want to.

The same idea is with a *Yid* who has to bring a *korban*. He really wants to bring it, but the *yetzer hara* may get in the way and say, "No! I don't want to bring the *korban*". What do we do? We force him to bring the *korban*! This really means, we are forcing his **yetzer hara** to get out of the way. We are not forcing the *Yid*, we are letting the *Yid* do what he really wants, his **true** will.

Lesson - Sometimes we want to do a *mitzva* but it seems hard for us. We may think, "How can I possibly do this *mitzva*, It's too hard...?" We need to realize that it's the *yetzer hara* who is trying to stop us! We really want to do all the *mitzvos*! We have to get the *yetzer hara* out of the way, and then we can easily do what we really want - the *mitzvos* of Hashem!

(Based on Gur Aryeh vayikra 1:3)

צַו

Just a Little Finger

The *Yidden* finished putting together all the *keilim* of the *mishkan*, and for seven days the Kohanim did the avoda and put up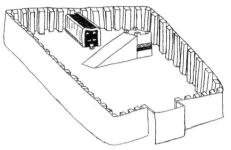

the *mishkan*. Finally on the eighth day Hashem's *Shechina* came down and rested in the *mishkan*.

Question - How is it possible that we, simple people, had the ability to bring the *Shechina* of Hashem all the way down into this world? Isn't our avoda unimportant compared to Hashem's greatness?

Answer - Although we are so far from Hashem's greatness and our *avoda* alone doesn't deserve to bring the *Shechina* down. Still, Hashem wants us to do our part, and Hashem considers our small deeds very great. Even great enough to bring the *Shechina* down!

The following story brings out this idea. Rabbi Chanina ben Dosa once found a large stone and wanted

to bring it to the *Beis Hamikdash*, but he couldn't carry it by himself. Suddenly *malochim* appeared and said that they can carry it for him but on one condition, he needs to help by at least putting his finger on the stone. He did so and suddenly he found himself standing, with the stone, in front of the *Beis Hamikdash*!

All he needed to do was something small and the rest was all done on its own.

In a similar way with the building of the *mishkan*, Hashem wanted us to put our effort, and considered it as if we did something very great, and we were able to bring the *Shechina* down!

Lesson - When we do a *mitzva* we should always remember how great it is in the eyes Hashem. No matter how small it may seem, like just 'putting a finger', it is precious to Hashem and He considers it as something big. It is our actions that will bring the  *Shechina* down again, in the third *Beis Hamikdash*!

(See Farbrengen 11 nisan 5732)

61

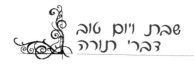

⟨☀ חַג הַפֶּסַח ☀⟩

Leaving Egypt Today

בְּכָל דוֹר וָדוֹר חַיָּיב אָדָם לִרְאוֹת
אֶת עַצְמוֹ כְּאִילוּ הוּא יָצָא מִמִּצְרָיִם:

This means, that even today we have to feel as if we ourselves went out of *Mitzrayim*.

Question - How is that possible, we were never slaves in *Mitzrayim*?!

Answer - In *Mitzrayim* the *Mitzri* said to the *Yid*, "Get to work! Serve Paroh!" The *Yid* would say, "No, I don't want to!" when the *Yid* went out of *Mitzrayim* he told the *Mitzri*, "I will not serve Paroh, I will serve Hashem!"

Now in *golus* we face a similar challenge. The *yetzer hara* is like the *Mitzri*, he tells us, "Work for the *yetzer hara*! Don't look in your siddur when you *bentch*! Don't say the *possuk* of *chumash*!" The *neshama* says, "No! I **want** to look in my siddur! I **want** to learn *chumash*! I **want** to serve Hashem!"

Just like by *yetzias Mitzrayim* the *Yid* said, "I'm not listening to you! I'm not serving Paroh anymore! I only serve Hashem!" So too now, we have to "go out of *Mitzrayim*" by telling the *yetzer hara*, "I'm not listening to you! "I WILL look in my siddur! I WILL learn *chumash*! I am going to serve Hashem!"

(Based on Tanya perek 47; 11 nisan 5728)

 שְׁמִינִי

To Help a Fellow Yid

After the seven days of practicing the avoda in the mishkan, "בַּיּוֹם הַשְּׁמִינִי," on the eighth day, the Yidden were waiting for the Shechina to come down and rest in the mishkan.

In whose zechus will the Shechina come down? You would probably think it would be in the zechus of Moshe, the greatest of all the Yidden. But in fact, Moshe told Aharon, "Hashem chose you! In honor of **your** korbanos the Shechina will come down!"

Question – Moshe was the leader of the generation and the greatest person in his time, shouldn't the Shechina have come down in **his** zechus?

Answer – Every mitzva that we do brings us closer to Hashem. The difference between Moshe and Aharon was:

Moshe, gave us the Torah from Hashem and taught us **what** the mitzvos are.

Aharon, helped the *Yidden* **actually do** the *mitzvos* and come close to Hashem. If a *Yid* had a hard time doing any of the *mitzvos*, he would talk to him and guide him in a friendly way **making it possible** for him too to do the *mitzvos* and connect to Hashem.

When it came time to bring the *Shechina* down to the *mishkan* and **connect the Yidden** to Hashem, Hashem said it will be in the *zechus* of Aharon. Since he was the one who would always find a way to bring the *Yidden* close to Hashem.

Lesson – In these last generations before the *geula*, we saw that when the Rebbe'im had a choice whether to spend their time learning *Torah* or to bring *Yidden* closer to *Yidd*ishkeit, they chose to focus on bringing *Yidden* closer to *Torah* and *mitzvos*. Because they knew that this is the dearest to Hashem and this will bring the *Shechina* down again in the third *Beis Hamikdash*.

(Based on sicha shabbos Parshas Shmini 5732)

תַזְרִיעַ

Sensitivity

In this week's *parsha* we learn about the *tuma* of a *metzora*. This is a person who spoke *lashon hara* and Hashem put *tzora'as* (-white spots) on his skin. He shows the *tzora'as* to the *Kohen* and after the *Kohen* examines it he determines if he is *tomei* or not.

Question – All other *tumos* in the *Torah* don't need another person to determine if it's *tomei*, either you are *tomei* or not. Why then by a *metzora* do we need the assistance of a *Kohen* to determine if he is *tomei*?

Answer – The *tuma* of a *metzora* is different than all other *tumos*. The *metzora* is sent out of all three of the *Yiddishe* camps. He has to sit alone, he can't cut his hair, he must tear his clothes and many other *halachos*.

Who has the right to make this big decision? Only a *Kohen*! As we know, Aharon was an אִישׁ הַחֶסֶד, a kind

66

man. He truly felt the pain of the other person as if it was his own.

When a metzora would come to him, before deciding to make him *tomei* he would be extra careful, he would double and triple check, "Is he really *tomei*, can I actually send him out of the *Yiddishe* camp?" Only then would he announce him to be *tomei*. That is why by this *tuma* the *Torah* says that only a *Kohen*, who loves every *Yid*, could announce it.

Lesson - Sometimes we see someone doing something wrong and we might want to tell the teacher. We learn from *Parshas Metzora*, that we should instead try to act like Aharon Ha*kohen* who only looked at the good in others and tried to help them do better.

(Based on Likutei Sichos vol. 27 p. 88)

מְצוֹרָע

Part of One Body

After the days that the *metzora* was sent out of the *Yiddishe* camp, *Parshas Metzora* teaches us the way he becomes pure. One of the things he has to do is bring a קרבן to Hashem.

The *Gemara* says that if a person wants, he can volunteer to bring the *korban* on behalf of a *metzora*, and the *metzora* will be forgiven through these *korbanos!*

Question – How is this allowed? If the *metzora* is the one who needs the forgiveness and has to bring the *korban*, how can a **different** person bring the *korban* for him?

Answer – The reason why it is possible for one *Yid* to bring a *korban* for another *Yid* is because, " כָּל יִשְׂרָאֵל עֲרֵבִים זֶה לָזֶה", every *Yid* is connected, and responsible, for his fellow *Yid*. Therefore, when one *Yid* becomes a *metzora* and needs to become pure, every *Yid* who is really **a part of him** is able to help. Since he isn't a separate

person, but rather he is connected to him, he can even bring a *korban* **for him!**

Lesson – This teaches is a tremendous lesson in *ahavas Yisroel*. All *Yidden* are like one body consisting of many parts. When one *Yid* is experiencing something good, like a *simcha*, or he won a prize, we feel his joy and are happy with him, since we are part of the same body. The same thing is true when something not good happens to another *Yid*, for example, someone gets hurt *chas veshalom* or loses a game, we feel his pain and aren't happy until that *Yid* is happy too!

(Based on Likutei Sichos vol. 27 p. 101)

A New Person

In *Parshas Acharei* we learn about the holiest day of the year, *Yom Kippur*. The *parsha* describes how the *Kohen Gadol* would enter the *kodesh hakodoshim* to do the special *avoda*.

One of the *mitzvos* is that when the *Kohen Gadol* did the *Yom Kippur avoda,* he would wear *bigdei lavan*, special white clothes. After *Yom Kippur*, the *Torah* commands the *Kohen Gadol* to put away the *bigdei lavan* and they cannot be used again. Every year the *Kohen Gadol* needs to buy a new set of *bigdei lavan.*

Question - What is the reason for this interesting *halacha*? All other *bigdei kehuna* were allowed to be used more than just one time. Why are the *bigdei lavan* different?

Answer - The reason why the garments of *Yom Kippur* have to be new each year is to show us how great the *teshuva* of *Yom Kippur* is. What *teshuva* accomplishes is not just that a *Yid* is forgiven for his sin, but rather after a *Yid* does *teshuva* properly, he becomes a **completely different person**. He is now a person who does *mitzvos*, and has nothing to do with the aveiros that he did before.

To bring out this point, every year when the *Kohen Gadol* comes to do the *avoda* of *Yom Kippur*, the *Torah* tells him to wear **brand new clothes** to show us that through *teshuva* we become a new person!

Lesson - Our mission in this world is to do only *mitzvos*, but even if *chas veshalom* we did an *aveira* we must know that through *teshuva* we have the ability to forget the past and become a completely new person! A person who **only** does the *mitzvos* of Hashem!

(Based on Likutei Sichos vol. 28 p. 224)

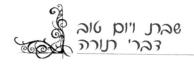

קְדוֹשִׁים

Make Yourself at Home

In *Parshas Kedoshim* we learn about the *mitzvos* connected to the first years of a new tree:

- The first three years are עׇרְלָה – the fruits cannot be eaten.

- The fourth year is called נֶטַע רְבָעִי – these fruits are eaten in *Yerusholayim*.

- In the fifth year you may eat its fruit at home, and Hashem will give a *beracha,* "לְהוֹסִיף לָכֶם תְּבוּאָתוֹ" that your produce will be plentiful!

The whole purpose of why Hashem wants us to do this *mitzva* for four years is to lead up to the "לְהוֹסִיף לָכֶם" **in order** that we can get the *beracha* in the fifth year. This shows us that the fifth year is even greater than the previous four years.

Question – If the fifth year is even greater than the previous four years, why is the **fourth** year called holy and has to be eaten in *Yerusholayim*, while the **fifth** year can be eaten at home?

72

Answer – Hashem gave us the *Torah* and *mitzvos* with the purpose to make **this world** a דִּירָה בְּתַחְתּוֹנִים - a dwelling place for Hashem. The *neshama* leaves *Gan Eden* and comes down to this world to serve Hashem, because Hashem wants the *neshama* to be in a physical world and take physical things and use them for Hashem.

Based on this we could understand why the fifth year of the tree is the greatest year and is the purpose of all the previous years. The purpose is not to stay in *Yerusholayim*, like staying in *Gan Eden*, but rather to take the fruits to your regular home and use it **there** to serve Hashem!

Lesson - In every part of our day we can serve Hashem. Not just when we are doing *ruchniyus* (spiritual) things like *davening* and learning, but even when we are doing regular physical things like eating or playing. When we make a *beracha,* and play with *ahavas Yisroel* then we use our physical things to make a dwelling place for Hashem.

(Based on Likutei Sichos vol. 7 p. 134)

73

שבת ויום טוב
דברי תורה

⤝ אֱמוֹר ⤞

Don't Tell

At the end of *Parshas Emor* we learn about a *Yid* who got very angry and רַחֲמָנָא לִיצְלַן cursed Hashem's name! The *Yidden* were shocked and didn't know what to do. They locked him up in prison and asked Moshe what has to be done. While he was waiting in prison Moshe

asked Hashem what to do. Hashem told Moshe that this *Yid* should be stoned to death.

There was also a different time when the *Yidden* had a question for Moshe, by *Pesach Sheini*. There were *Yidden* who were *tomei* and were not allowed to bring the *korban Pesach*. They turned to Moshe asking for a chance to bring the *korban Pesach*. Moshe told them, "Wait right here! Let me ask Hashem for an answer right away!"

Question - Why is it that when the *Yidden* had a question by *Pesach Sheini* Moshe *Rabeinu* rushed to get them an answer from Hashem, but when the *Yidden* had a question about the *Yid* who cursed Hashem, Moshe

Rabeinu was in no rush and had him wait in prison until he got an answer?

Answer - Moshe *Rabeinu* truly loved every *Yid*, as we see that Moshe even *davened* for the *Yidden* who served *avoda zara* by the חֵטְא הָעֵגֶל!

By *Pesach Sheini* when the *Yidden* were asking Moshe for something good, for another *mitzva*, for that Moshe *Rabeinu* **rushed** to get them an answer right away. But when it came to finding a punishment for a *Yid*, Moshe was in no rush. Let the *Yid* live a little longer and when Hashem decides he will let me know what has to be done.

Lesson - Just like Moshe *Rabeinu*, the Rebbe shows us to take every opportunity to speak good about another *Yid*, to find something positive about them. We should do the same and always try to use every opportunity to only bring good to a fellow *Yid*.

(Based on Toras Menachem 5726 vol. 3 p. 234)

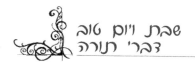

A Little Big

This week's *parsha* begins by saying that 'ה spoke to Moshe "בְּהַר סִינַי", On the Mountain of Sinai.

The reason why the *Torah* was given on Har Sinai and not on the other mountains, was because while the other mountains were showing off how they were bigger and taller, little Har Sinai stood there humble, not showing off its height and greatness. It was on this mountain that Hashem chose to give the *Torah*.

The Question remains - If Hashem wanted to teach us a lesson to be humble, He shouldn't have given the *Torah* on **any** mountain, not even a small one. He should have given the *Torah* in a valley, that would be truly humble! Furthermore, the name of the *parsha* is - בְּהַר! Stressing the point of a **mountain**.

Answer - It is true that a *Yid* must always be humble, at the same time we also need to be like a mountain and 'stand up tall'. When is that? When we are performing *Torah* and *mitzvos* we must do it with *Yiddishe* pride and confidence. Even if we are being challenged by people around us, we must not be affected by them, and do the *mitzvos* proudly. So both are true, we must be **humble** in our mind not to be a show-off. But when it comes time to do a *mitzva* we do it with **pride** and **confidence** - proud to be a *Yid* and do Hashem's *mitzvos*!

Lesson - We live in a world with many different people around us. We may sometimes be doing a *mitzva* and feel uncomfortable about what the people around us may be thinking. *Parshas* בְּהַר teaches us to be proud like a mountain, to show the world that we are Hashem's nation and we are lucky and proud to keep His *Torah* and *mitzvos*!

(Based on Likutei Sichos vol. 22 p. 159)

בְּחוּקוֹתַי - חֲזַק

To End with a Bang!

This week we finish *Chumash Vayikra*. The rule is that the ending of a book or *sefer* brings out the point of the entire *sefer*.

Chumash Vayikra speaks about all the different *korbanos*. The end of *Parshas Bechukosai* speaks about the *korban maaser* - when a person has ten animals, he makes the tenth one *heilik* and brings it as a *korban* to Hashem. With this we end *Sefer Vayikra*.

Question – In general, there are two types of *korbanos*:

1) *Korbanos* that are made *heilik* by a person, like *Korban maaser*.

2) *Korbanos* that are made *heilik* by Hashem, like a *korban bechor* (-first born animal) which is made *heilik* by Hashem right when the animal is born.

Why does *chumash vayikra* end with *korban maaser*, which is made *heilik* by a person? Shouldn't the

ending and main point of all the *korbanos* be an even greater *korban*, one that is chosen by **Hashem**?

Answer - *Korban maaser* is the main point of all *korbanos*, specifically **because** it was made *heilik* by the *Yid* himself. Since the whole reason Hashem created this world was in order that a person should put in **his** effort, not just to rely on what is done **for him**. The point is that **we** should do *mitzvos*, and that **we** should make things *heilik*.

This also gives us excitement in what we are doing when we know that it is 'our project'.

Lesson - When we have a task in front of us at home or in school, for example, the table needs to be cleaned or our brother needs help, we can either wait until our father or our teacher tells us to do it, or we can jump ahead and do it on our own. When we do it on our own, it is much more precious to Hashem and we feel much more excited about it, since it was **our** idea and we did it!

(Based on Likutei Sichos vol. 17 p. 332)

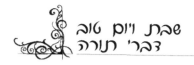

בְּמִדְבַּר

Finding the Gem

During the second year that the Yidden were in the midbar, Hashem commanded Moshe to count the Yidden for the third time.

Rashi asks: "Why does Hashem count the Yidden so many times?" He answers: "Hashem keeps counting the Yidden in order to show how precious they are to Him", just like someone who keeps counting his treasures again and again since they are so precious to him.

Question – Hashem already knew the number of Yidden before He counted them, so why did Hashem ever need to count them in the first place?

Answer - The "precious gem" in every Yid is his pure *neshama*, "the פִּינטעלע אִיד". This spark is always connected to Hashem and empowers a Yid to do everything he can to do what Hashem wants.

Sometimes the *yetzer hara* and one's *aveiros* can cover over this "precious gem" preventing a *Yid* from feeling his close connection to Hashem. Hashem **counts** the *Yidden* to let **us** know how precious we really are. This makes our "gem" shine so that we can feel our connection to Hashem and do His *mitzvos* in a better way. Every time we *lein* this *parsha* it is like Hashem counts us again.

Lesson – We are always connected to Hashem; yet, if we don't do the *mitzvos* properly, we may not feel this connection. A *Yid*, however, wants to always feel Hashem! All we have to do is uncover our gem. We accomplish this by learning more *Torah* and being more careful with the *mitzvos*. Then, we will surely feel closer to Hashem.

(See Likutei Sichos vol. 8 p. 209)

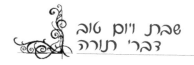

✠ חַג הַשָּׁבוּעוֹת ✠

Echo Echo Echo Echo

One of the names of *Shavuos* is זְמַן מַתַּן תּוֹרָתֵינוּ, since on this day Hashem gave us the *Torah*.

The *Midrash* tells us that by *matan Torah* Hashem's voice reached the whole world, yet it did not make an echo.

Question – Sounds create echoes when they bounce off a wall or mountain, just like a ball bounces off a wall. The louder the voice is, the greater the echo will be. Hashem's voice reached the whole world, so why did it not produce an echo?

Answer – At *matan Torah*, the *Torah* and *mitzvos* that came from Hashem didn't stay in *shomayim*, but actually became **part of the world.** The world absorbed them and they became connected to the *Yidden*. The

82

Torah and *mitzvos* didn't "**bounce off**", therefore, Hashem's voice did not have an echo.

After *matan Torah*, physical objects are able to absorb *kedusha*.

Whenever we do a *mitzva* with physical things, for example, wool used to make tzitzis or paper to write words of *Torah*, we bring *kedusha* into them.

(Based on Likutei Sichos vol. 4 p. 1092)

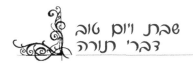

חַג הַשָּׁבוּעוֹת (ב)

Wake up!

It took 49 days from when the *Yidden* left *Mitzrayim* until *matan Torah*. The *Midrash* tells us that these were days of preparation, after which the *Yidden* were ready to receive the *Torah*.

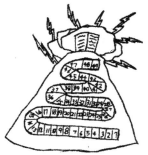

In the morning of *matan Torah*, Hashem came down to Har Sinai, but the *Yidden* were not there! Moshe went and found them sleeping in their tents. Hashem was not happy about this. To make up for the *Yidden*'s mistake, every year we stay up the night of *Shavuos* and learn *Torah*.

Question – If you were going on an exciting trip, would you be able to sleep the night before? How then were the *Yidden* able to sleep, especially after 49 days of excited anticipation?

Answer - The *Yidden* went to sleep because they knew that all their preparation for *matan Torah* could not compare to what the *neshama* could accomplish while asleep. When a *Yid* sleeps, the *neshama* goes up to *shomayim* and is much closer to Hashem. After preparing for 49 days in this world, the *Yidden* wanted to get even closer to Hashem. They did this by going to sleep, so their *neshama* could become even more *heilik*.

Question - If so, why was Hashem upset? Didn't the *Yidden* do a good thing by going to sleep?

Answer - Hashem created the *neshama* and put it in a physical body, so that we should serve Him **here** in **this** world. Hashem doesn't want us to leave this world, rather serve Him the best we can with our physical bodies. Hashem was upset when the *Yidden* got ready for *matan Torah* by going to sleep, because they should have stayed awake -in this world- instead of going up to *shomayim*.

(Based on Likutei Sichos vol. 4 p. 1024)

נָשֹׂא

Every Inch Counts

In this week's *parsha*, we learn about the donations that the twelve *Nesiim* gave towards the *mishkan*. One of the donations was six wagons, four of which carried the *kerashim* (the large beams of wood used in the walls of the  mishkan). The *Gemara* adds that the beams just barely fit into the four wagons.

Question – Had there been more wagons, it would've been easier to fit the *kerashim* in them. Why then were only four wagons donated for carrying the *kerashim*, when the *Nesiim* could have given more?

Answer - When giving *tzedaka*, extra is often better. On the other hand, when it came to the building of the *mishkan*, the donations had to be exact. Everything was used out to its full capacity. Had the *Nesiim* given more than four wagons, there would have been extra space that would not have been used!

Lesson - One may say, "I serve Hashem so many hours a day, I *daven*, and I learn in Yeshiva. It's okay if I waste a little time and don't serve Hashem a small part of the day." We learn from the *mishkan*, that every single moment in our lives is for the purpose of serving Hashem to our full capacity. We cannot miss even one moment!

(Based on Likutei Sichos vol. 28 p. 40)

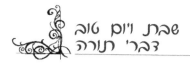

בְּהַעֲלֹתְךָ

Why not?!

In this week's *parsha* we learn about the *korban Pesach* offered the first year in the *midbar*. Rashi explains that this was the **only** *korban Pesach* the *Yidden* made the entire forty years that they were in the *midbar!* It was considered shameful that the *Yidden* didn't bring a *korban Pesach* for all those years.

Question - Hashem only commanded the *Yidden* to bring the *korban Pesach* the first year they were in the *midbar*. There was no *mitzva* to bring this *korban* in the following years. If so, why was it considered shameful that they didn't bring the *korban Pesach* the other years?

Answer - Although the *Yidden* were only commanded to bring this single *korban Pesach*, they should have learned a lesson from the story of *Pesach Sheini* (also mentioned in this week's *parsha*). By the story of *Pesach Sheini* the *Yidden* who were *tomei* were not able to bring the *korban Pesach*. They could have just said, "Oh

88

well, we're *tomei* and we don't have the *mitzva* of bringing the *korban Pesach*." They didn't say that, rather, they complained to Moshe, "We know that we don't **need** to bring a *korban Pesach*, but **why should we lose out on this *mitzva*, לָמָּה נִגָּרַע**?!"

Although Hashem didn't ask for a *korban Pesach* after the first year, the *Yidden* should have stood up and complained, "**לָמָּה נִגָּרַע**?! Why should we lose out, we want to do **another** *mitzva*!"

Lesson - As children in Hashem's army, we are very excited to do more and more of Hashem's *mitzvos*. Sometimes we have an opportunity to do a *mitzva* that we don't have to do, like picking up a classmate's pencil when it drops. Whenever you have a chance to do another *mitzva* - grab it!

(Based on Likutei Sichos vol. 23 p. 65)

שֶׁלַח

We can do It!

The *Yidden* were ready to enter *Eretz Yisroel*. Before entering, Moshe sent spies to check out the land. Moshe told them, "Go and find out what kind of land it is? Are its people strong or weak...?" and many other details.

When the spies returned they reported: "The people that live in the land are strong, and so are their cities." "Therefore," the spies concluded, "We are unable to fight the people, since they are stronger than us!"

Their report caused the *Yidden* to cry out, "We don't want to enter *Eretz Yisroel*! We would rather return to *Mitzrayim*!" Seeing this, Hashem punished the *Yidden* to stay in the desert for forty years, and the ten spies died right away in a plague.

Question - What did the spies do wrong? Didn't Moshe ask them to check out the land and report those

90

very details? Why were the spies, and all the *Yidden*, punished?

Answer - The sin of the spies was not in their **report**, but rather in the **conclusion** they made: "We are unable to win over them". Moshe had told them to see what is the best **way** to conquer the land, not **if** we can conquer it. If Hashem told us to conquer the land of course we are able to!

Lesson - When Hashem commands us to do a *mitzva*, (like the *mitzva* of conquering *Eretz Kanaan*,) He also gives us the *koach* and ability to do it. No *mitzva* can be too hard for us to fulfil. If we feel that a *mitzva* is too difficult and we can't do it, then we know who that fear is coming from - the *yetzer hara*. He is trying, like the *meraglim*, to tell us that we are unable to do what Hashem wants. We must therefore ignore the *yetzer hara* and listen to our little "Moshe *Rabeinu*", the *yetzer tov*, and immediately do Hashem's *mitzvos!*

(Based on Likutei Sichos vol. 13 p. 39)

91

קֹרַח

Forget and Forgive

Korach went and gathered Dasan, Aviram, with 250 people and convinced them to rebel against Moshe. They came to Moshe and said, "Why did you make yourself the leader and chose your brother Aharon to be the *Kohen Gadol?!* We also want to be leaders!"

Hashem was not happy and told Moshe that he wants to destroy them all. Moshe told Hashem, "Only one person sinned and you get angry at everyone?!" Hashem answered Moshe, "I know, and I will let everyone know who the real sinners are!"

Question - What did Moshe mean when he said, "Only one person sinned..."? There were many people who sinned?

Answer - Moshe was saying, "I know that many *Yidden* sinned, but they don't really mean it, they are only ganging up because of one person - Korach! He is causing the whole argument!" Hashem answered Moshe that He will not punish everyone, but there are still *Yidden* who are sinners on their own, like Dasan and Aviram, and they too deserve to die.

Lesson - Just imagine, only a few *pesukim* earlier Dasan and Aviram spoke really disrespectful to Moshe. Ever since they left *Mitzrayim*, and even in *Mitzrayim*, they gave Moshe a real hard time. Yet, when Hashem wanted to punish Dasan and Aviram, Moshe said, "They're not the real sinners, let them live!"

This teaches us how much love to have for every *Yid*, even for someone who acts not nicely to us. This is called אַהֲבַת חִנָם, loving a *Yid* for no reason. It is this *mitzva* that will bring *Moshiach* now!

(Based on Likutei Sichos vol. 13 p.51)

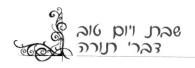

חֻקַּת

But it's not my Job!

In the year before the *Yidden* entered *Eretz Yisroel* two great *Yidden* passed away: Aharon Ha*kohen* and Miriam *Haneviah*. The *Torah* tells us that after Miriam passed away the well that the *Yidden* drank from stopped giving water. And when Aharon passed away the "עֲנַנֵי הַכָּבוֹד", the clouds that protected the *Yidden*, left them. Later on, these two miracles came back in the *zechus* of Moshe.

Question - The *Torah* isn't a story book; each part of the *Torah* teaches us a lesson. What lesson can we learn from this part of the *Torah*?

Answer - The reason why these two miracles stopped after Aharon and Miriam passed away, was because the clouds and the well were only there in their *zechus*.

The clouds - were in the *zechus* of Aharon. Since Aharon loved every single *Yid* **equally**, without making a difference between one *Yid* and another, whether he was a *tzadik* or *chas veshalom* a rasha. In his *zechus* Hashem gave the *Yidden* the protecting clouds, which **surrounded** all the *Yidden* **equally**.

The well - was in the *zechus* of Miriam. Since Miriam (together with her mother) took care of the **small children** in *Mitzrayim*. In her *zechus* Hashem gave the *Yidden* water, since the nature of water is to go down to the **lowest heights** (-similar to children who are **small in height**).

After they passed away, Moshe took over their "job", their way of serving Hashem, and brought back these two miracles.

Lesson - When the *Yidden* needed water and protection (now that the well and clouds left them), Moshe took over Aharon and Miriam's job, even though it wasn't **his** job and way of serving Hashem. So too us, if our mother or our teacher asks us to do something, instead of saying, "But it's not my job!" or, "I don't like doing it!" We learn from Moshe to answer, "If it has  to get done, then I'm doing it, even if it's not my job or style."

(Based on Likutei Sichos vol. 2 p. 331)

95

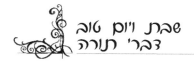

בָּלָק

Who Started?

Balak was frightened that the *Yidden* would kill out his nation. He therefore called Bilam Harasha to curse the *Yidden* for him. In the end, instead of cursing the *Yidden*, Bilam gave them many great *berachos*.

Question - The name of a *parsha* shows us what the *parsha* is all about. If so, shouldn't the name of this week's *parsha* be *Parshas Bilam* not *Balak*, since most of the *parsha* speaks about **Bilam's** journey, and how his plans were turned around?

Answer - It is true that Bilam is the main character in the *parsha*, at the same time, who was the one who started it all? Who was the one who hired Bilam to curse the *Yidden*? It was Balak! Since he is the one who gave the

idea to curse the *Yidden*, the entire *parsha* is named after **him**.

Lesson - We learn from here how what we say to others can be so powerful. For example, if we think of something good to do and get our friends to do it, we might think that we didn't really do anything special, we only **thought** of the idea, but didn't actually do it. The *Torah* teaches us that just **thinking** of an idea and getting others to do it, is considered **our credit**!!

(Based on sicha shabbos Parshas Balak 5733)

פִּינְחָס

A Loving Family

In the end of last week's *parsha* the *Yidden* were dying in a plague for marrying the daughters of *Midyan* and serving *avoda zara*. Zimri, the leader of *shevet* Shimon, went and married a *Midyan* girl in front of Moshe, the *Zekeinim* and all the *Yidden* and nobody knew what to do. Pinchas jumped up and said, "I remember the *halacha*!" He took a spear and killed Zimri together with the *Midyan* girl. It was only then that the *Yidden* finally stopped dying.

Question - How is it that the young Pinchas remembered what to do when Moshe and the *Zekeinim* did not remember? And from where did he get the strength to risk his life by killing the leader of a *shevet*, knowing that the whole *shevet* might want to kill him?

Answer - The *Torah* answers this question right at the beginning of our *parsha*: "פִּינְחָס בֶּן אֶלְעָזָר בֶּן אַהֲרֹן הַכֹּהֵן", the *Torah* tells us that Pinchas is the grandson of Aharon.

Aharon was the one who had tremendous love for all the *Yidden* and always made peace between them. He was also the one who stood up to Paroh demanding to set the *Yidden* free.

Pinchas, as a grandson of Aharon, also had this tremendous love for the *Yidden*. When he saw the *Yidden* dying one after another he frantically searched for a way to stop it. This strong desire of his to save the *Yidden* caused him to firstly, remember the *halacha* that everyone else had forgotten, and secondly, risk his life to fulfill the *halacha*, in order to stop the plague!

Lesson - This is an important lesson for us especially in the days between *shiva asar b'Tamuz* and *tisha b'Av*. The *Beis Hamikdash* was destroyed because of the opposite of *ahavas Yisroel*, let us do our best to take a lesson from Pinchas to have such great *ahavas Yisroel* and do whatever we can to help another *Yid*, even if it may be hard for us. For example, if we are playing and we see a kid standing on the side we make sure to include him in our team, even if he isn't the  best at the game. This will surely bring the third *Beis Hamikdash* with the coming of *Moshiach*.

(Based on Toras Menachem 5748 vol. 4 p. 71)

⫷ מַטּוֹת-מַסְעֵי ⫸

Mark the Date!

In *Parshas Masei* we learn about the Passing of Aharon Ha*kohen*. The *Torah* says that he passed away on the first day of the fifth month, which is *Menachem Av*.

Question - The *Torah* doesn't record the date of the passing of anyone else, why does the *Torah* record the date of Aharon's passing?

Answer - There is a connection between Aharon's passing and the date when he passed away. The month of *av* is the month of the destruction of both the first and second *Beis Hamikdash*, on *tisha b'Av*. The passing of Aharon is connected to *tisha b'Av* in two ways:

1) The *Gemara* says that the day that a *tzadik* passes away is equal to the destruction of the *Beis*

Hamikdash. If so, the day of Aharon's passing is connected to *tisha b'Av*.

2) The reason why the *Beis Hamikdash* was destroyed was because of the **opposite** of *ahavas Yisroel*. And the way we will merit to have the third *Beis Hamikdash* rebuilt is by having extra *ahavas Yisroel*. Aharon Ha*kohen*, as we know, had tremendous *ahavas Yisroel* for every *Yid* - which is the key to the **rebuilding** of the *Beis Hamikdash*. It is for these two reasons that the *Torah* records the date of Aharon's passing.

Rosh Chodesh av, the *Yahrtzeit* of Aharon, is a special day for us to take a lesson from Aharon's way of life and strengthen our *ahavas Yisroel*. Through this we will merit to have the rebuilding of the third *Beis Hamikdash*!

(Based on Likutei Sichos vol. 18 p. 411)

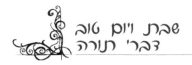

☒ דְּבָרִים - שַׁבָּת חֲזוֹן ☒

A Peek from a Distance

There was once a father who bought his son a beautiful suit. The son was very excited with his gift and wore it proudly.

One day, the boy went outside to play wearing his new suit. He was not careful and the suit got all dirty and torn. His father was very upset. Yet, he went and bought his son a second new suit.

Time passed, and the boy went outside again to play wearing the second suit. Once again, he was not careful, and... this suit tore as well! This time the father went and bought his son a third suit, but didn't give it to him right away. Instead, he put the suit away and told his son that when his behavior will improve he will earn it.

Every now and then the father would take out the suit, show it to his son and say, "This suit will be yours, when your behavior will be fit to receive it." The boy really wanted to get the suit, so he improved his behavior until finally his father felt he was ready to receive the suit.

≈

Reb Levi Yitzchak of *Berditchev* told this story as a *mashal* for the *Yidden* and the *Beis Hamikdash*. He explained:

Hashem gave us the first *Beis Hamikdash*, but, unfortunately, through our sins the *Beis Hamikdash* was destroyed. Hashem gave us the second *Beis Hamikdash*, but this *Beis Hamikdash* too was destroyed through our sins. Then Hashem prepared the third *Beis Hamikdash*, but did not give it to us right away, He is keeping it hidden away in *shomayim*. Hashem is waiting for us to do *teshuva* and be deserving of it. It is then that He will finally give us the gift - the third *Beis Hamikdash*!

Just like in the *mashal*, there is a time when Hashem shows us the third *Beis Hamikdash*. When is this? On *shabbos chazon*! *Chazon* means a vision; on this *shabbos*, Hashem gives us a "vision", a peek, of the third *Beis Hamikdash*. Hashem hopes that by showing us the third *Beis Hamikdash* we, Hashem's children, will 'improve our behavior' and do *teshuva* to be worthy of it.

Let us show Hashem that **we are ready**! We hope that this year we will finally earn 'the gift' and get to see the third *Beis Hamikdash*, not just in a vision, but in reality, in the holy city of *Yerusholayim*, *amein*!

(Based on Likutei Sichos vol. 9 p. 24)

שבת ו'ום טוב
דברי תורה

וָאֶתְחַנַּן

Don't Stop Breathing!

In this week's *parsha* the *Torah* tells us about the importance of reviewing the *Torah* that we learn. The *Torah* says, "Just be careful and watch your life well, so that you do not forget the things that you saw... at *Har Sinai*." The *chachomim* learn from here that if someone forgets something that he learned, he is responsible for his life (חייב מיתה)!

Question - Why is forgetting *Torah* considered such a big sin, that if someone forgets something they learned they deserve such a big punishment like losing their life?

Answer - *Torah* is our life, therefore, *chas veshalom* stopping to learn or forgetting *Torah* - which is our life - causes us **automatically** to lose our life *chas veshalom*. It is not a punishment, but rather a direct outcome from our actions.

Lesson - Just like we can't stop eating or breathing even for just one day, so too, we always have to learn - and review- the *Torah* every day. Even during vacation days when we are not in school, we continue to learn *Torah* since it is our life!

104

The following story brings out this point:

In the times of Rabbi Akiva, the Romans made a decree not allowing *Yidden* to learn or teach *Torah*. Rabbi Akiva still continued teaching *Torah*, even in public! A student asked him how could he risk his life and continue teaching *Torah*? Rabbi Akiva answered him with a story about a hungry fox that came to the water and saw some fish swimming back and forth with very worried looking faces. The fox asked the fish what they were worried about. They answered that that day the fishermen were out to catch them, so they're trying to escape the fishermen! The sly fox advised the fish, "Why don't you come here to the dry land and I will protect you from the fishermen!" The fish answered, "Fool! The water is our life, we can't live without water. If we stay in the water we have a chance to survive, but if we come out to the dry land we will **surely** die!

So too, explained Rabbi Akiva, is with the *Yidden* and the *Torah*. The *Torah* is our life; the Romans may or may not 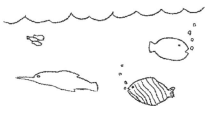 take away my life for learning *Torah*, but if I **stop** learning *Torah chas veshalom*, I will surely lose my life!

(Based on Likutei Sichos vol. 34 p. 31)

עֵקֶב

The Final Reward

In the beginning of *Parshas Eikev* Moshe *Rabeinu* tells the *Yidden* about the rewards they will receive for doing the *mitzvos*. Moshe said, "Hashem will bless you, your children, your fruits, your grain,
your wine etc." and lists many *gashmiyus'dike* (-material) *berachos* that the *Yidden* will get.

Question - When we do something good and get rewarded for it, the reward matches the action that earned it. Now *mitzvos*, which are the will of Hashem, are much greater than *gashmiyus'dike* things like fruits and grain. If so, how is it possible that the reward for doing *mitzvos* is these *gashmiyus'dike* things?!

Answer - The reward for doing *mitzvos* is actually **not** the *gashmiyus'dike* things. The *Mishna* says that, "שָׂכַר מִצְוָה מִצְוָה", the reward for a *mitzva* is the *mitzva* itself. This means that the greatest reward a *Yid* can get for doing a *mitzva* is this itself that he is doing a *mitzva*

and connecting to Hashem. When we do what Hashem wants -His *mitzvos*- that connects us to Him. **That** is the greatest reward!

In addition, "מִצְוָה גּוֹרֶרֶת מִצְוָה", by doing one *mitzva*, we will get to do yet **another** *mitzva* and make another connection to Hashem!

So what are all the *gashmiyus'dike berachos* about? All the *gashmiyus* that Hashem promises us is just in order to make it easier for us to do **more** *mitzvos*. Since, when we have all the *berachos* that we need then we have no worries and can easily perform Hashem's *mitzvos*.

Lesson - When we do a *mitzva* we should remember that we are connecting to Hashem. The more *mitzvos* we do the more connected to Hashem we will be! Knowing this will give us a true excitement every time we get to do another *mitzva*, knowing that this is the greatest fortune!

(Based on Sefer Hasichos 5749 vol. 4 p. 163)

107

✡ רְאֵה - אֱלוּל ✡

The King in the Field

There was once a great king who ruled over many countries. Those who wanted to meet him needed special permission and had to wait many months. Even then, only very important people and ministers would get the privilege to see the king.

One day, the king made an announcement that he would be leaving his big beautiful palace for a full month. He would go out to an open field where everyone could greet him and ask for whatever they want. When the people in the country heard this they were so excited to be able to get a chance to meet the king.

When the time came, the king came out to the field. He greeted each person with a smile and gave them whatever they asked for.

When the month was over, everyone followed the king back to his palace where he allowed only his ministers to enter with him.

≈

This story is a *mashal* about the *Yidden* and Hashem. Hashem is our king and we are His nation. During the year it isn't always easy to ask Hashem for what we want. There are many conditions on when and how to ask and who deserves to be answered. In the month of *Elul*, when Hashem is much closer to us, He greets us with a happy face and we can ask for whatever we want. When *Rosh Hashana* comes, Hashem goes back into "His palace". Then only those who serve Hashem properly can enter into the palace with Him.

In this month we blow the shofar, do *teshuva* and ask Hashem to help us serve Him better. Through this, we become like the king's "close ministers" on *Rosh Hashana*, and we can ask Hashem for whatever we need. We especially ask for what we need the most – *Moshiach* now!

(Based on Likutei Torah Parshas Re'ei p. 32)

כתיבה וחתימה טובה
לשנה טובה ומתוקה!

שׁוֹפְטִים

Don't Judge!

This week's *parsha* begins with the words, "שׁוֹפְטִים וְשׁוֹטְרִים תִּתֶּן לְךָ בְּכָל שְׁעָרֶיךָ", "You should appoint judges and officers in all your gates." This applies even outside of *Eretz Yisroel*.

Later in the *parsha* we learn about the *mitzva* of עִיר מִקְלָט. If a *Yid* - *chas veshalom* - mistakenly kills another *Yid*, he must run to one of the special cities that were set aside. There, the relatives of the killed person could not kill him. These cities were only set aside in *Eretz Yisroel*. If someone killed another person outside *Eretz Yisroel*, he will only be safe if he flees to an עִיר מִקְלָט in *Eretz Yisroel*.

Question – Why do judges and officers have to be in all cities, even outside *Eretz Yisroel*, but the cities of עִיר מִקְלָט are only in *Eretz Yisroel*?

Answer - The *Yid* who killed another person must run to an עִיר מִקְלָט because he needs to do *teshuva* and become more *heilik*. The right place to become *heilik* is specifically in *Eretz Yisroel*. The judges, however, are there to jdge the *Yidden* in their day-to-day life - when a *halacha* question arises, when a business disagreement occurs between two people, etc. To be able to best understand and help the *Yidden*, the judges and officers need to live in the same city as them.

Lesson - Before judging someone we must first "put ourselves in their place" to fully understand their situation like the judges who needed to live in the same place as the people they were judging.

If we see a friend in a bad mood, instead of thinking bad thoughts about him, first try to understand why he's acting this way. Perhaps he woke up late and missed his ride to school, or maybe he didn't have breakfast that morning. If we think in such a way, we will always think nicely about each other and have many friends. In addition, now in *chodesh Elul*, Hashem will judge **us** favorably and give us a כְּתִיבָה וַחֲתִימָה טוֹבָה!

(Based on Likutei Sichos vol. 2 p. 380)

111

כִּי תֵצֵא

We're on Top!

This week's *parsha* begins with the words, " כִּי תֵצֵא לַמִלְחָמָה עַל אֹיְבֶיךָ," "When you will go out to war over your enemies..." There are many different *mitzvos* in the *parsha* about going to war.

chabad.org   www.Chabad.org/Parsha

Questions:

1) Shouldn't the *Torah* have said, " כִּי תֵצֵא לַמִלְחָמָה עַם אֹיְבֶיךָ," "When you will go out to war **with** your enemies," not **over**?

2) Every lesson in the *Torah* applies to us **today**. Since we are not going to war, what could the lesson of this week's *parsha* be for us?

Answer - This *possuk* is talking about the war with our **true** enemy - the *yetzer hara*! He harms us when he gets us to do an *aveira*.

A child might get worried and say, "How can I fight the *yetzer hara*, he is much stronger than me?" The *Torah*

tells us, when you go out to fight the *yetzer hara*, "עַל אוֹיְבֶיךָ" we start out already "**over** your enemy!" A *Yid* has the upper hand because Hashem is on our side. We have nothing to worry about for we are surely going to win!

(Based on Likutei Sichos vol. 2 p. 384; p. 697)

כִּי תָבוֹא

Wait, I'm not There Yet!

This week's *parsha* tells us about the *mitzva* of *bikurim*. When the *Yidden* will enter *Eretz Yisroel* and plant their fields, they will bring the first and best fruits as an offering to Hashem.

Rashi tells us that this *mitzva* was not performed until after fourteen years when **all** the *Yidden* finished fighting their enemies and settled in *Eretz Yisroel*.

Question - Many *Yidden* settled down before the fourteen years passed, why didn't they fulfill the *mitzva* and bring their *bikurim* then?

Answer - A *Yid* who lives in a home cannot have complete happiness when he knows of another *Yid* who isn't settled yet. The *Torah* tells us that the *mitzva* of bikurim has to be performed with *simcha*, in a joyous way.

114

To feel this true happiness, the *Yidden* waited until every last one settled in their home.

Lesson - When playing with a fun game or toy while some kids are standing on the side watching, we could either continue playing or

include them. What we learn from the *mitzva* of *bikurim* is to include others in our joy. Then we enjoy our game with even more fun.

(Based on Likutei Sichos vol. 9 p. 155)

נִצָּבִים

The Secret to a Good Year

Parshas Nitzavim is always read the *shabbos* before *Rosh Hashana*. The הקדוש של"ה says that each Yom Tov has a special connection to the *parsha* of that week.

Question - What is the connection between *Rosh Hashana* and *Parshas Nitzavim?*

Answer - *Parshas Nitzavim* starts off with the words, "אַתֶּם נִצָּבִים הַיּוֹם כֻּלְּכֶם לִפְנֵי ה' אֱלֹקֵיכֶם", "You are all standing today before Hashem." The Alter Rebbe explains that the word "הַיּוֹם - **today**" refers to the special day of *Rosh Hashana.*

Moshe *Rabeinu* tells the *Yidden* that the key to be successful in the judgment of, הַיּוֹם, *Rosh Hashana* is by, "אַתֶּם נִצָּבִים הַיּוֹם כֻּלְּכֶם" by "**standing all together as one**"

with **achdus**. Even though all *Yidden* are different from each other, they should unite as one.

Reading this *parsha* before *Rosh Hashana* gives us the *koach* and ability to be *b'achdus* so we can be *zoche* to a שנה טובה ומתוקה.

(Based on Likutei Sichos vol. 2 p. 398)

117

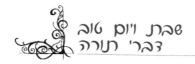

☀ רֹאשׁ הַשָּׁנָה ☀

It's all in the Head

The Yom Tov *Rosh Hashana* has four names: 1) רֹאשׁ הַשָּׁנָה 2) יוֹם תְּרוּעָה (3 and 4) יוֹם הַזִּכָּרוֹן (3 הַדִּין. Each name expresses a different point. רֹאשׁ הַשָּׁנָה means "head of the year". It is called by this because this day is the beginning of the new year.

Question - If this day is the first day of the year, shouldn't the name have been "תְּחִלַּת הַשָּׁנָה" which means the **beginning** of the year?!

Answer - The name רֹאשׁ הַשָּׁנָה actually teaches us that this day is not only the day that **begins** the year, but actually greatly affects the whole upcoming year.

Just like the head of a person controls and brings life to the whole body, *Rosh Hashana* controls and brings life to the whole year. The way we behave on *Rosh Hashana* influences the rest of the year.

We should, therefore, be very careful to *daven* with extra *kavana* and say *Tehillim* every extra moment we have.

On *Rosh Hashana*, we have special customs that we do in honor of the new year. We eat pomegranates with their many seeds, so that we should have many merits. We also dip apple in honey to have a sweet new year.

Doing these things ensure that we will have a good, sweet and healthy year! Hashem will surely  *bentch* us with all the *berachos* we need.

(Based on Igros Kodesh 1st day of selichos 5710)

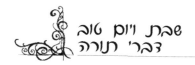

וַיֵּלֶךְ:

A Message from the King

In this *parsha*, Moishe tells the *Yidden* about the *mitzva* of *hakhel*. In the year following שְׁמִיטָה, during the Yom Tov of *Sukkos*, all the *Yidden* gather together in the *Beis Hamikdash* where the *Yiddishe* king would read to them certain parts of *Chumash Devarim*.

Question - *Beis din* were the ones who would teach the *Yidden Torah*. If so, why did the **king** read the *Torah* to the *Yidden* and not the **beis din**?

Answer - Not everyone is at the same level in terms of their learning of *Torah*. Some people can learn Chumash, some *Mishnayos*, while others are able to learn *Gemara*. The *beis din* needs to teach each *Yid* according to his level. The gathering together of the *Yidden* for *hakhel* was not to **teach** the *Yidden Torah*, rather to awaken their *neshama* and their **connection to Hashem** for the coming years. In this, everyone is equal, from the

greatest *talmid chacham* to the simplest *Yid*, they all have the same pure *neshama* and connection to Hashem.

The king takes care of and **unites all the *Yidden* together**, thus he was chosen to read the *Torah* for the *mitzva* of *hakhel*. Since it is then, that the king inspires the *neshama* and connection to 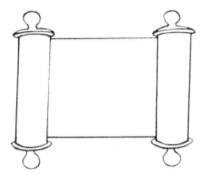 Hashem in which all *Yidden* are **equal** and **unite as one**.

(Based on Likutei Sichos vol. 19 p. 301; p. 369)

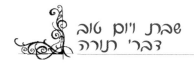

☙ הַאֲזִינוּ ☙

Hold on Tight

This week's *parsha* includes the special song called "שִׁירַת הַאֲזִינוּ". The Leviim would sing this שִׁירָה every *shabbos* when the Kohanim would bring the *korban musaf*.

In one of the *pesukim* of שִׁירַת הַאֲזִינוּ it says, "יַעֲקֹב חֶבֶל נַחֲלָתוֹ - Yaakov (the *Yidden*) is Hashem's portion". The word חֶבֶל also means a rope. This means that the *Yidden* are called Hashem's "rope".

Question - Why are the *Yidden* compared to a rope?

Answer - When two people are holding a rope at each end and one of them pulls, the person on the other end comes along too. The same is with Hashem and the *Yidden*. If we do an *aveira, chas veshalom*, we are not just lowering ourselves down, we are actually lowering Hashem down too, רַחֲמָנָא לִיצְלַן!

A rope can also show us something good. This "rope" that connects us to Hashem, gives us the *koach* and possibility to always do *teshuva*. "אַף עַל פִּי שֶׁחָטָא יִשְׂרָאֵל
הוּא", even when someone sins, before doing *teshuva*, he is still connected to Hashem. We are never too low nor 'stuck' *chas veshalom* because we always have this connection with Hashem to give us the power and push to do *teshuva*.

(Based on Likutei Sichos vol. 9 p. 215)

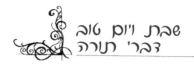

⊠ חַג הַסֻּכּוֹת ⊠

Because we're Different

One of the *mitzvos* we do on *Sukkos* is the *mitzva* of shaking the *arba minim* (four types). They are: *lulav, esrog, hadasim* and *aravos*.

What is the reason behind this special *mitzva*?

The *Midrash* explains that this *mitzva* is a sign how all the *Yidden* should unite together. The *arba minim* represent all four types of *Yidden*.

Esrog – has a good **smell** and a good **taste**. This represents the *Yid* who learns *Torah* and does **mitzvos**.

Lulav – comes from a date tree. Dates have a good **taste** but have no smell. This represents the *Yid* who learns *Torah* but doesn't focus as much on the *mitzvos*.

Hadasim – have a good **smell** but no taste. This represents the *Yid* who does *mitzvos* but doesn't focus as much on learning *Torah*.

 Aravos – have no taste and no smell. This represents the *Yid* who does not focus **not** on the *mitzvos* and **not** on learning *Torah*.

We tie all the four types together to show that all the *Yidden* should unite as one. Even if we are different from each other, we don't think the same or act the same as our friends do, still, we learn from the *mitzva* of lulav that we can, and we **will** all unite as one!

(Based on Likutei Sichos vol. 4 p. 1159)

125

שִׂמְחַת תּוֹרָה

My Torah!

On *Simchas Torah* we dance with the *Torah* to celebrate the yearly conclusion of reading the entire *Torah*. Every *shabbos* we *lein* one *parsha* and on Simchas *Torah* we finish the last *parsha* – V'zos Haberacha.

Question - Why do we celebrate and dance with the *Torah* now that it's finished and not on *Shavuos* when we received the *Torah* from Hashem for the very first time?

Answer - On *Shavuos* we celebrate receiving the *Torah* as a **gift** from Hashem. Our joy for the *Torah* cannot be complete until we **learn** it. Once we make a *siyum* of the whole *Torah* on Simchas *Torah*, then we can be truly happy. When we put effort into learning the *Torah*, and complete it, it becomes "our *Torah*"!

Story - A *chossid* once came to the Tzemach Tzedek and complained that he has no excitement nor desire to learn. The Tzemach Tzedek answered him, "What should I do that I **do** have a desire to learn?" The true simcha in *Torah* comes when we put our effort into it.

Let us take a *hachlata* that we will put extra effort into our learning this coming year, so that we will make the *Torah* ours!

(Based on Likutei Sichos vol. 14 p. 156)

שבת ו"ום טוב
דברי תורה

Let's Review...

What does this week's *parsha* speak about?

_____

_____

_____

What question do we have?

_____

_____

_____

What is the answer?

_____

_____

_____

What lesson can we learn from this week's *parsha*?

_____

_____

_____

מוקדש
לכ"ק אדמו"ר נשיא דורנו
שנזכה להתגלותו תיכף ומיד

לזכות
אבי מורי הרב חיים לוי
ואמי מורתי מרת בילא רישא שיחיו
גאלדשטיין

ולזכות

חמי הר' אהרן חיים
וחמותי מרת ברכה שיחיו
וואלף

שתהי' להם בריאות הנכונה לאויוש"ט, ולנחת
חסידית מכל יוצאי חלציהם כן ירבו

Made in the USA
Middletown, DE
26 February 2022